CLOSE!
CLOSE!
CLOSE!

HOW TO MAKE THE SALE

John Fenton

Pfeiffer
& COMPANY

Amsterdam • Johannesburg • London
San Diego • Sydney • Toronto

Publisher: Pfeiffer/Mercury Books
Published in the UK by Mercury Books.
This edition published by:
    Pfeiffer & Company
    8517 Production Avenue
    San Diego, CA 92121-2280 USA
    (619) 578-5900   Fax (619) 578-2042

This publication is designed to provide accurate and authoritative information in regard to the subject matter covered. It is sold with the understanding that the publisher is not engaged in rendering legal, accounting, or other professional service. If legal advice or other expert assistance is required, the services of a competent professional person should be sought. *From a Declaration of Principles jointly adopted by a Committee of the American Bar Association and a Committee of Publishers.*

Editors: JoAnn Padgett, Katharine Munson
Page Compositor: Nicola Ruskin
Cover: John Odam Design Associates

Library of Congress Cataloging-in-Publication Data
Fenton, John
        Close! close! close! / John Fenton.
              p.   cm.
        Includes index.
        ISBN 0-89384-217-6
        1. Selling. 2. Sales management.   I. Title.
        HF5438.25.F454   1993
        658.8'5 — dc20   92-50994

Printed in the United States of America.
Printing 1 2 3 4 5 6 7 8 9 10

Contents

". . .nothing happens until somebody
sells something!"

John Fenton

"If you don't *close,* you're working for
the competition!"

Alfred Tack

"Almost every buying decision has some negative aspects from the customer's point of view,
and these have to be overcome through the use
of an appropriate closing technique."

Heinz M. Goldmann

"You haven't done your job if you quit without
asking for the order at least five times."

J. Douglas Edwards

"In selling, our income and achievement
depends almost entirely on our ability to *close.*"

Robin Fielder

In every survey ever conducted asking sales managers what
skill they would most like to increase in their salespeople,
closing has always emerged as the clear winner.

1

Can You Succeed in Selling Without Being a Good Closer?

The short answer is no, you can't. The long answer begins with why such a question was asked in the first place. And the answer to *that* is because there are so many salespeople out there who can't close, who don't close, who forget to close, who are terrified of closing, who are paranoid about being turned down and won't put themselves in the turndown-risk situation, who are so negative they expect a "No" before they even start selling—"You don't want any more widgets this month, I suppose, do you?"

This book is for all those salespeople who feel closing is unreal, not for them, not necessary in their business, unethical, high pressure, and too complicated.

This book is also for all those professional salespeople who have already recognized that closing is for real, forever, and very necessary, and who want to be even better at it than they are now—and *richer!*

Closing is *not* high pressure. Closing is *not* unethical. If you are being paid to sell and you *don't* close, you are taking money under false pretenses. That's stealing! That's fraud! If you are being paid to sell and you don't close, you are working for the competition (we'll explain how and why, later). That's treason!

In this first chapter I am going to convince you, with the aid of logic, facts and statistics, survey results, and *proof*, that you cannot survive in selling without closing.

Pressure

Let's sympathize with all those thousands of salespeople who think that when you use a closing technique, you are applying *pressure* to the customer.

What is a closing technique? It is anything you can ethically do or say that gets you closer to the decision to buy. For example:

Salesperson: "Are you happy with everything?" (Pause.)

Customer: "Uh, yyyess, I think so."

Salesperson: "Fine. Can we go ahead?" (Shut up.)

This must be about the simplest pair of questions you can ask a customer at the end of a good sales presentation. All doubts are clarified. All questions are answered. A direct "Will you buy?" then close.

As every salesperson knows, after the second question— "Can we go ahead?"—you *shut up*. And that's when the pressure starts in this job.

That's why we said, "Let's sympathize with all of those thousands of salespeople..." because they haven't even got this bit right.

Where is the pressure? Think about it. Sure, the pressure is in the silence, but all the customer is doing during those few seconds of silence is mulling things over: "Should I, shouldn't I? Seems okay. Solves our problem. Can't see any snags. Why not? Okay." That's how the customer's mind is working.

So who's sweating? You are. The pressure is on *you*, not on the customer. It's unbearable. And after three seconds of that silence you open your big mouth and ruin the customer's train of thought.

Ethics

Professional salespeople don't beat up old ladies. Professional salespeople don't do the following:

- Put their feet in the door.
- Seduce the customer's assistant.

- Grab the customer's tie and tighten the knot until they get a "Yes."
- Knock their competitors.
- Keep selling after they've established that no need exists for their product or service.
- Keep selling after they've established that the customer cannot afford to buy.

And professional salespeople don't lie. They don't mislead or misrepresent. They don't exaggerate or give deliberately optimistic delivery dates. They don't promise future delights and rewards that they know will never exist. They don't oversell.

However, strictly in the interest of furthering good customer relations, all salespeople are allowed three teeny-weeny white lies.

1. "You're right."
2. "It's my fault."
3. "It's been a pleasure to meet you."

The One-in-Five Survey

A comprehensive survey was conducted by The Institute of Purchasing Management in Great Britain. The survey covered all kinds of people who buy things—purchasing managers, production managers, office managers, executives, and the whole range of decision makers. It established beyond any doubt that

Only one in five customers will ever volunteer an order.

The other four out of five expect the salesperson to ask for an order. If the salesperson doesn't ask, he or she goes away empty-handed. Believe it. It's true.

So, statistically, those salespeople who *never close,* who never ask for the order, don't even have a chance with 80 percent of the business. Their market, their *total* market, is an insignificant 20 percent of the total market that good closers can benefit from.

Of course, you never know which of any five customers is the one who will volunteer an order. So, the only logical thing to do with this situation is

Never let a potential order go unasked for.

The 8/73 Survey

Another piece of relevant international research on both salespeople and their customers is known as the 8/73 Survey. The main research was conducted to find out how salespeople reacted to objections from customers. An objection is a doubt in the customer's mind that is voiced: something the customer is not sure about, is worried about, is not clear about, or doesn't like about the proposal.

Rarely will a salesperson sail smoothly through a sales presentation, from the opening thirty seconds to writing up the order, without encountering a single objection. Things are simply not that easy.

Objections are like hurdles in a race: you know they're going to be there, you know you've got to get over them, you know what direction you're running in, and you know where the finish line is. Your only problem is physical. Can you get over all the hurdles and reach the finish line before you run out of steam? The answer will be a measure of your fitness, your fitness to sell the particular products or services that you are responsible for.

And in the selling profession your fitness is a direct measure of your *knowledge* and how you use it. That knowledge falls into seven categories:

- Product Knowledge
- Application Knowledge
- Financial Knowledge
- Knowledge of Your Customer's Business
- Knowledge of Your Customer's Markets
- Knowledge of Your Competitors
- Knowledge of Selling Techniques

Many customers are not direct about voicing their doubts, and they need to be encouraged. Otherwise they bottle them up and the salesperson, when closing time arrives, gets a "No" in response to the first attempt to ask for the order. And many salespeople faced with this "No" mentally breathe a big sigh of relief and escape as fast as possible, convincing themselves that they've done the best they can.

Wrong! Wrong! Wrong!

Nine times out of ten that "No" wasn't a real "No"; it was the customer's way of saying, "I'm not quite sure yet." And a "No, not yet" is very different from a "No, not ever."

This is the simplest way to deal with that first "No."

"Is there something you're still not sure about?" (Pause, two, three.)

The customer starts telling you the doubt. Listen, deal with it, then ask for the order again.

"Are you happy with everything now? Can we go ahead?"

Any more doubts will come out easily and can be dealt with following the same pattern. Close again. Hurdles, hurdles, hurdles!

Back to the 8/73 Survey. For the purpose of presenting the figures, all "No's" are classified as "No, not yets": that is, objections based on a doubt. Research into the reaction of salespeople to the objections they received from their customers revealed:

- 44 percent gave up after the first objection.
- 22 percent gave up after the second objection.
- 16 percent gave up after the third objection.
- 10 percent gave up after the fourth objection.

So, 92 percent gave up after four objections, leaving only 8 percent of the salespeople still selling. That's the "8" part of the 8/73 Survey.

The "73" part comes from the second half of the research. This half asked customers to discuss the kind and the quantity of objections they voiced to their salespeople.

The kind of objections pinpointed are not relevant here, but the quantity is. The research established that 73 percent of customers voiced *five or more* objections before being sure enough to place an order.

So, there you have it. These two parts of the survey prove that 8 percent of salespeople will win 73 percent of the business. Good odds if you are among the eight percent.

In fact, the situation is significantly worse than this, because both the 92 percent of salespeople who gave up and the 8 percent still going after four objections are the salespeople who actually got as far as asking for the order *at least once*. The salespeople who don't close at all aren't even in the race.

The Best Closers

Now I'm going to hit you where it *really* hurts. Smack in your ego! Who are the best closers? Who are the people who never give up, who never take no for an answer? Answer: children between the ages of six and nine.

Maybe it's happened to you. Maybe you've seen it happen to some other parent. Visualize a sunny Sunday morning in the park, just before lunch.

"Dad, can I have an ice cream cone?"

"No. It's too near your lunchtime."

"Oh, come on, Dad. Just a little one."

"*No*. I've already told you."

"Oh, please, Dad. I want one."

"*No*. That's enough."

(Tears and fifty more decibels.) "I wanna ice creeeeeamm."

"Okay...okay... But don't tell your mother."

Children *never* give up. Why is that? It's because before the age of nine their conditioning hasn't taken effect. Think about it. All through your life, through your early childhood, through school, through early adulthood and your first tastes of business

Whatever you wanted to do, someone, somewhere, always said "No!"

We are all thoroughly conditioned to expect "No." Is it any wonder that it's always been so difficult coming to grips with closing a sale? We are trying to change the world.

Apart from learning the techniques that I'm going to teach you so that you become a great closer (these will be covered indepth later in the book), all you have to do is change your normal built-in "No" expectation into a "Yes" expectation, just like that child in the park. Every time you feel yourself chickening out at the end of a sales presentation, just remember that kids aged six to nine are much better at it than you. Then let your ego take over. How much has your education and training cost since you were that good? What a waste!

Remember, too, your greatest ally: the bumblebee. Aero-dynamically, it is impossible for the bumblebee to fly—that huge, heavy, hairy body; those tiny wings.

But nobody ever told the bumblebee!

One final thing to remember when you're feeling timid about closing a sale:

No one has ever been struck by lightning asking for an order.

Not one fatality has ever been recorded when closing the sale. It is one of the safest things to do on God's earth.

Can you succeed in selling without being a good closer? No, you can't. A British film called *Reluctant Heroes*—what a perfect name for novice salespeople—featured the catch phrase:

I can, I must, and I will.

That you *can* is not in doubt, is it? It is not a physical impossibility for you to open your mouth and ask for an order.

That you *must* is demonstrated by the results of the two pieces of research we've just discussed: the One-in-Five Survey and the 8/73 Survey. Are you a dummy or an intelligent human being?

That you will is dependent on how well your ego, your pride, and your self-esteem combine to overcome your conditioning and make you want to be better than six- to nine-year-old kids in the job you've been trained for and are paid to do.

2

Excuses and Autopsy Checklists*

For sales managers, vice presidents, and directors of sales only. Salespeople should move directly to Chapter 3.

I want to put a question to all of the sales managers, vice presidents, and directors of sales who are reading this book. Have you ever analyzed your salespeoples' call reports over, say, a six-month period to pinpoint the kind of excuses they give for not getting an order? Note, *"excuses,"* not reasons!

At our company Structured Training, we've done this many times for many clients. As a result, and without breaking any confidences, we can present our own universal Top Ten Excuses for not closing.

The customer

1. Wants to think it over for a few days.
2. Wants to get other bids.
3. Doesn't want to spend that kind of money.
4. Wants a steeper discount than we can give.
5. Wants to stick with his or her usual supplier.
6. Needs it by next week, and we can't deliver for four weeks.
7. Doesn't think enough of his or her customers will buy it.
8. Feels it is too much trouble to switch vendors.
9. Feels it is too complicated for his or her people.
10. Was too busy to listen carefully.

Do any of these ten strike responsive chords? Do any bring back memories of last week or last month?

There are many ways to eliminate, or at least minimize, these kinds of excuses for not closing, but more on this later. First, let's consider three more things that will stop you from getting the order, three that you will never in a million years see on any salesperson's call report. These are our Top Three Reasons (not excuses) for losing the order.

1. I messed up the demonstration.
2. I offended the customer by: arriving twenty minutes late; not having the right support materials; smoking in the office; smelling like a brewery; dressing unprofessionally.

And the last reason eclipses all of the other twelve rolled into one:

3. I DIDN'T ASK FOR THE ORDER.

I will deal with the Top Three Reasons comprehensively later in the book. To eliminate your salespeople's versions of the Top Ten Excuses, all you need are some Autopsy Checklists (ACs). (See sample AC on p.15.)

Every time you see an excuse on a call report, hand the salesperson the appropriate AC and ask him or her to complete it. ACs are a form of remedial training and people soon catch on. Doing the job right in the first place is much easier than having to complete the AC later.

Autopsy Checklist

EXCUSE: The customer wants to think it over for a few days.

Why does he or she want to think it over?

What specifically does he or she want to think over?

How many specific doubts does he or she still have?

Why does he or she still have **any** doubts after you've given your full presentation?

What research, proof, or testimonials can you give to clear up any doubts?

How many of these proofs did you use during your presentation?

Did you actually *ask* for the order?

How many times?

How did you **ask**? What were the exact words you used?

When are you going back to see the customer?

Write out below IN DETAIL what you are going to say that will give you the best chance of winning the order.

Have this AC completed and on my desk by 3:00 p.m. tomorrow.

(Your Name and Title)

3

How to Help Customers Make Up Their Minds

There are many different reasons why customers will say "Yes" to a deal. In his book *The Super Salesman's Handbook*, William Davis lists a number of them, and I would like to elaborate on some of his points.

1. They want to own what you have to offer.

   This is the easiest close. You have a desirable product and have managed to convince the customer of that fact.

2. They think it will benefit their company.

   Again, you have done a good job. You have demonstrated the benefits of the product, proving the existence of a favorable cost/benefit ratio.

3. They fear that if they don't buy now, they will have to pay more later on.

   You have successfully generated a sense of urgency by worrying the customer about the risk of a price increase next month.

4. They can't resist the word "New."

   New has always been the best word to use in selling. Even today it still works magic. Telling a customer that you have a new brochure or a new product will often open doors that would not open for yet another meeting about the same old product.

5. They like spending money.

   While this is unusual, don't ever underestimate that old chestnut about keeping up with the Joneses. Some people are determined to beat the Joneses. And sometimes at the very top end of a luxury market, prospective customers may like to think they are "pampering themselves" with your product.

6. They like you.

Most really successful salespeople are likeable. However, because not everyone likes the same sort of people, no one can rely on just a winning smile to get through every time.

7. They are not happy with their present suppliers and want to change.

You may simply have arrived at the right place at the right time with the right deal. Or the customer might have contacted you. Whichever, your assurances are going to be of paramount importance. Break one promise and you're dead.

8. They are in a hurry.

If this is the case, it is another lucky break for you, and not one that can be planned for. Find out why, and offer absolutely no discount.

9. They think it will make them look good.

Peer-group motivation is very important to all of us. If you can convince prospective customers that their bosses and peers will be impressed by the savings your product can generate, or by the terms of the deal you are offering, they will be more likely to buy.

10. They want to take advantage of discounts.

It's all a question of how you present the deal. Just don't start with the discount. That's not selling; it's giving money away.

11. They like making bold decisions.

If you're up against the dominant buyer, who is as cocky as they come, positive, and loves innovation, maybe this time *you* should display caution—but only until you have worked out this customer's cost/benefit ratio twice, just to be sure.

12. They have heard that a rival has done well with your product or service.

The use of referrals and word of mouth can never be beaten. It means that you come to the meeting with an advantage because the prospective customer is already eager to buy. If the sale falls through, you should seriously consider following another career.

13. They don't have the courage to say "No."

But don't oversell or overstock. All you'll get later are rejections; you'll never get face to face again. The customer won't risk it.

14. They are greedy.

And you have been able to stimulate this greed by painting pictures of future profits or ways to squeeze out a rival.

15. They feel insecure.

And you have a strong case for added security.

16. They need, or think they need, your product or service.

If they have already identified a need, you simply have to convince them that yours is the right product for them.

17. They are happy or in the right mood.

Lucky you! But remember, luck isn't an abstract; it's a place—the place where preparation meets opportunity.

18. They are afraid that someone else will beat them to it.

The Joneses again! This could be a fear that you have planted in their minds, or it could be there already waiting for you to build upon it.

Why People Say "No"

It's not all going to come up smelling like roses. William Davis also has a list of reasons why people say "No."

1. They haven't been listening.

   One of our Top Ten Excuses for not closing, remember? It may or may not be your fault, but it's possible that these customers will listen next time if they are caught at a better moment.

2. They only wanted to find out if you had any good ideas.

   Or to check prices. If you do have some good ideas, then there is still an opportunity to follow up on whatever initial impression you have made. If you don't have any good ideas, you had better sit down with a pad and pencil and think of some.

3. They are prejudiced against your product.

   Find out why. Is it misinformation or bad past experience? Whichever, you have an opportunity to change their opinions with information, with explanation, and especially with referrals from other satisfied customers.

4. They don't like you.

   This could be a problem and if you can't crack it, it might be better to suggest that someone else on the team tries to follow up next time. If that person gets the same reaction, chances are it's the customer, not you.

5. They hate making decisions.

   Then you need to look for opportunities to help them make decisions.

6. They don't have the authority to make decisions.

   Then you know you have the wrong person and can find out who the right one is before making another call.

7. They haven't got the money.

There might be ways around that if the problem is looked at closely enough: for example, a payment plan extended over time or a leasing arrangement.

8. They are afraid of the consequences of saying "Yes."

In this case it is up to you to calm their fears, even if it takes several visits, demonstrations at other customer locations, guarantees, personal assurances, and, of course, a dozen third-party reference letters.

9. They are tired or in the wrong mood.

Again, this is just bad timing and another call on another day could easily produce an order. Prospective customers will presumably appreciate your sensitivity in leaving them alone when they don't feel like talking.

10. They don't like change.

If this is the case, they need to become accustomed to the idea of what the product or service will do for them, until they feel comfortable with it. Resistance to change is fear of the unknown. And often it is based on lethargy; it's too much trouble to change. Many businesses go broke every year due to this kind of lethargy.

11. They haven't understood your presentation.

Have you been talking in jargon? Regular open-ended questions will reveal this problem and then you can provide clarification.

12. They are misers.

If so, they need to be shown how much money they will save or make by investing in the product.

13. They are simply not convinced.

    Then you need to produce more evidence.

14. They know someone who will make a better offer.

    You need to show enough interest to find out who this person is and, if possible, what the offer is. If you can't top it, at least you will know more about what the competition is up to.

15. They hope you will come back and improve your terms.

    This is a tactic. After all, it is their job to get the best possible deal. You should certainly try again, provided it doesn't mean giving away too much.

16. They don't like the color, shape, or feel of your product.

    This doesn't sound like the real reason. Explore. Perhaps whatever they dislike can be changed or they can be convinced that the benefits outweigh the problems.

17. They are worried about your after-sales service.

    By demonstrating the degree of service that you are willing to put in and by proving that you have actually done so in the past, you will be able to build up their confidence in the company as a whole. You need to show that you are willing to take *personal* responsibility for their account, and that you don't think the job ends with the close.

18. Their wives or husbands won't let them say "Yes."

    Then the salesperson probably needs to meet the spouse in order to convince him or her as well.

New to the Job

Job changes within companies that are potential customers often present good opportunities for closing sales. First, there are the outgoing job holders. They no longer have to worry about getting into trouble for making decisions that might not follow current company policy or that mean a significant change in the traditional way of doing things. By the time the consequences of their actions are known, they will be safely out of the way. If they like you, and have been putting off making a decision because of caution, this might be the time to turn them around.

Second, newcomers to jobs are an even better bet. Whether they are newly recruited or newly promoted, people entering a decision-making role are always anxious to make their mark. They are receptive to ideas that will make them look good, and their superiors are usually happy to let them get on with the job for the first few months. A newly promoted or appointed executive also gives you the opportunity to resurrect proposals that were rejected by a predecessor.

Choosing Your Words

The words you use during the closing part of your presentation, and indeed all the way through it, can determine whether a "Yes" or "No" response is received.

Some words are good for closing and others are bad. Rather than ask someone to pay for your product, for instance, you should ask them to invest in it. By simply changing one word you are showing them that to say "Yes" would be a sensible move, a move that would make money, not cost money. Furthermore, you are arming them with words to use when justifying their decisions to peers or superiors.

Instead of asking them to *sign* a form, ask them to *okay* it. We all have a built-in fear of putting our names to things, particularly if there is small print involved, just in case we are signing away our lives. If we are asked to okay something, however, the other party is recognizing that we have a certain status and is asking us to be agreeable and helpful, which most of us are happy to be.

I have talked already about the power of the word "New," but it cannot be stressed too much. Architects, for instance, are notorious for disliking salespeople, but they love innovation. So if you call them to say you have a "new" design manual and you would like to give them their copy, you will be in. If you are displaying a new product at a trade show and you hang a large sign over the product with just that one word on it, you will immediately attract a crowd.

If you are setting an appointment by phone with a potentially hostile firm, emphasize the "new" angle and you will be in. A surprising number of companies fail to capitalize on this simple fact.

When talking to a prospective customer avoid vague words and phrases like "I wonder if" and replace them with "I'm sure that." All customers like to feel that the seller is confident of his or her subject and product. If you show any doubts or hesitancy they will be less willing to take a risk on your recommendation.

Try talking about *savings* rather than *costs*. The differences are obvious and there are often ways of reversing the two terms in a presentation.

The Possessive Technique

Try to make customers feel that the product is theirs as early in the sale as you can. This is achieved by using words like *you* and *your* as often as possible: "When *you* have been using *your* Universal Widget Crusher for a few weeks, *you'll* be amazed at how much *your* crushing costs have been reduced."

The Five Words That Really Turn Customers On

Research has shown that there are five words that always make customers sit up, listen, and remember after the salesperson has left.

- **Increase**
- **Improve**
- **Reduce**
- **Save**
- **Gain**

The more they are used—all of them—the better, both throughout the presentation and throughout the close.

4

How Many Closing Techniques Do You Need to Master?

To be a brilliant closer of sales, how many closing techniques do you need to have mastered, to have in your bag, ready to use when the opportunity presents itself?

The answer is six—that's all. Whether you are selling high tech to industry or products for resale to retailers—the number of closing techniques required to be a master closer is just six.

Again, research proved this: a survey of 100 successful high-tech salespeople and 100 successful retail salespeople revealed their favorite closes.

High-Tech Favorite Closes

Seventy-four percent of high-tech salespeople prefer the *Alternative Choice Close*. For example:

"Do you want us to do the installation or will your technical people do it?"

"Do you prefer the white finish or the satin aluminum?"

"Will you be paying cash or should we send an invoice?"

"Would you like us to deliver it or would you rather pick it up yourself?"

"Do you want delivery on Tuesdays or Thursdays?"

"I'm in your area next Tuesday. Can I come and see you in the morning or the afternoon?"

Nine percent of high-tech salespeople prefer the *Concession Close*. For example:

"If we can get you delivery a week earlier than normal, can I have your order today?"

"If I can get production to paint it your house color, do we have a deal?"

"If I can shave another 2 to 5 percent off the price, can we go ahead?"

Seven percent of high-tech salespeople, however, prefer the *Summary Close*, which is a particularly good weapon for overcoming the "I want to think it over" objection. For example:

"Let's review the things we've covered today in our proposal. We've covered the performance of the equipment, and I think you said that you and everyone else were more than happy on this point. Am I correct?"

"Yes."

"We've covered the issue of acceptance by your work force, and again everyone is pleased that the demonstrations were well received and that our operator-training program will cover everything you're looking for. Is this right?"

"Yes."

"We've covered start-up costs, and I think you agree that they are lower than any of the alternative solutions you've been considering…" (Raise eyebrows at customer.)

"Yes."

"And we've covered maintenance costs and our customer service to your total satisfaction, haven't we?"

"Yes."

"In fact, the cost/benefit analysis for the equipment shows you recoup your investment within a year—well within your budget. Have I covered everything?"

"I think so."

"Okay. Can we go ahead? Can you get me an order number so that I can get things moving today?"

Four percent of the high-tech salespeople in the survey prefer to use a *Fear Close* (which doesn't mean threatening to send the boys around the next day if an order is not forthcoming). Normally this means fear of future price increases. For example:

"We expect a 6 percent price increase next month. I can hold the price we've quoted until the end of this month, I think, but to be absolutely certain, it would be safer to get the order in today. How about it?"

Or:

"What would happen if you have a fire before you install all these replacement extinguishers? Tonight, for example? If you decide now, they'll be here this afternoon. Why tempt fate when we're this close?"

Three percent of the high-tech salespeople voted for the *Verbal Proof Story Close*:

"I can understand that you want to think this over, Mr. Smith. In fact, I had a similar situation a few months ago over at Universal Widgets. They had been using Snook's Oils for years and it took them a long time to decide to switch to us. But since they did, they have been able reduce their inventory by a third because of our twenty-four-hour delivery service. They've also gotten a much better product life span by using our special cutting oils. They estimate that overall they're saving about $4,800 a week. Look (produces third-party reference letter), this is what UW's warehouse manager said in a letter to us only last month. Would it help you to decide if I spoke with UW and took you over to talk to your counterpart there? Every week you think about it could be costing your company the same kind of money—$4,800 a week. That's nearly $250,000 a year! Or can we get something started today?"

Here we have a true, relevant story—with numbers—about someone with whom your prospective customer can identify. It's followed up with an offer to set up a meeting, then reinforced with talk of the kind of money being lost while the customer thinks about it and doesn't act. The finale is an Alternative Choice Close: do you want to schedule the meeting or give me the order now!

This is the winning combination for Verbal Proof closing. The chances are that the prospective customer will not take up the offer of a meeting but will be satisfied with the letter and the fact that you were confident enough to offer the meeting with the third party.

So, five different techniques received 97 percent of the votes in the survey.

- Alternative Choice
- Concession
- Summary
- Fear
- Verbal Proof

If you add one more, you probably have the best six. That sixth technique is simply:

- Come out and ask for the order

The best way is to use the *One-Two Close*:

"Are you happy with everything?"
"Uh, yyyess, I think so."
"Fine. Can we go ahead?"

And then, shut up!

Favorite Closes When Selling to Retailers

Selling to retailers calls for a different art than high-tech selling does. In this part of the survey, 64 percent of sales-people named the *Order-Form Close* as their preferred method. This is the nearest thing to an automatic close that any retail salesperson can get. It means having the order form out and ready in the clipboard from the moment you enter the store. It also means having a copy of last month's order on the left-hand side of the clipboard and the entire range of products printed on the order form.

You start by checking what is in the store's stockroom and then going to the shelves where the company's products are on display. This means that the amount of stock sold since the last visit and the amount left to sell are known quantities. With retailing moving at the speed it does these days, over-selling is one of the worst mistakes you can make.

You then suggest to the store manager that you walk around the store together. While you are doing this (and most managers will agree unless they are particularly busy), you refer to the order forms and to the goods on display, asking questions as you go along.

"How's the new line moving? Is it as good as I said it would be? Great! Same again this month, or would you like to increase it to six cases?"

"Is this line still slow? It's going to pick up, don't worry. We've got an advertising campaign starting next week. It would be a good idea to fill the shelf in preparation. Shall I put you down for two cases?"

"We've got a special offer this month on this line. It will be making a big splash over the next few weeks. Do you think four cases would be enough?"

When you have been through every relevant line on the order form, plus any new lines that have not previously been discussed with the manager, make a final check on the form, show it to the manager, and say:

"Fine, I think we've covered everything. Would you just OK this for me as usual, here at the bottom?"

The next favorite, with 16 percent, is the Alternative Choice Close.

"Would you like six cases or eight?"

"Shall we deliver it all this week or would you rather take some of it next week?"

The Summary Close received 8 percent of the vote, the Fear Close 6 percent, and the Concession Close 4 percent.

That gives 98 percent to just five closes. If you add the "Just come out and ask for the order" Close, you have covered most situations and selling styles.

Remember what I said in Chapter 1:

No one has ever been struck by lightning asking for an order.

Closing a sale has never caused a fatality; it is one of the safest pastimes in the world.

Remember also the ABC of selling:

Always Be Closing.

Two Additional Key Closing Tools

1. The Most Powerful Question in Selling

This is a question that you can ask at the beginning of each sale in a number of different ways.

Let's assume that you have done some research and found that a particular company uses widgets, but you haven't been able to establish any more tangible objective than wanting to sell this company some of your widgets. You make contact with the key decision maker, preferably face-to-face, but by telephone will do, and you say:

"Good morning, Mr. Jones. As I understand it, your company uses a lot of widgets." (Pause.) "My company sells widgets. Very good ones. I'd like to see you using some of ours. May I ask you a very direct question?" (Here it comes.)

"What do I need to do to get you to buy some of your widgets from us?"

There are some variations on the same theme, such as:

"What do we need to do to get on your list of approved suppliers?"

Then, confirm the suggestion and ask for commitment:

"Okay. If we can do that, will you be ready to place an order with us?"

As you become more proficient at competitive selling, you will find that those three words—"if we can"—will unlock more doors than you ever thought possible.

You could also attempt to quantify the business:

"How much of your business will you be able to give us?"

"How soon?"

"What sizes?"

Then, provided you do what is suggested, to the manager's complete satisfaction, the business will be yours.

2. Starting With a Close

Why waste time on a long sales presentation if you can close the sale immediately? Obviously you have to start with a few preliminaries, such as "How do you do?" and "My name is John Fenton," but you could then go straight into the *Suppose Test Close:*

"Suppose you like me... Suppose you like the product...Suppose the price is acceptable... Suppose you like everything... Are you ready to buy today?"

If the answer is "Yes" or "I could be" then you know that you have a serious prospect and you can go after the business. If the answer is "No" or "I doubt it," you've got some more work to do in order to get your prospective customer to ready to buy. That could be easy or it could be hard.

Now read on.

5

Making Sure
the Customer
Is *Ready* to Be
Closed

Successful closing is not just something that ends a sale. It cannot be separated from successful selling. In order to maximize the chances of receiving a "Yes" and minimize the chances of a "No," you need to create an environment that is conducive to a successful close. This means that from the moment you come into contact with the customer you must start setting the mood. You don't necessarily have to ask for the order the moment you walk in the door, but you do have to start "conditioning" the customer to say "Yes" from the word go. You both need to be thinking that a close is likely all the way through the presentation. Remember to follow the Six P Principle: **Proper planning prevents possible poor performance.**

You need two basic plans. First, the *strategy*. This is the medium- to long-term plan for how to achieve the overall objectives. Strategy is about tomorrow. What are the objectives with this customer in developing the account? Second, the *tactics*. This is the short-term plan for how to achieve each specific objective. Tactics are about today.

Many salespeople can see the forest (strategy) and the trees (tactics) individually, but fail to see both together. Both plans must be flexible, since they need to be able to grow with the customer. Strategy and tactics need to be organic.

Don't Make Assumptions

A common mistake in these early stages is to make assumptions. This is very dangerous. Too many salespeople assume, for instance, that they don't have to plan in order to close.

Some assume that because a customer has agreed to see them, they are automatically going to make a sale. They become complacent, not selling themselves, their company,

or their products. They are then often amazed to find themselves leaving without the order.

Others assume that the customer likes the competition
better than them. This defeatist attitude means they are beaten
before they start. It is seldom based on any rational thinking
and is just a gut-level inferiority complex.

Some assume that the buying decision can't be made
today, so they leave without asking. What evidence do they
have for assuming that?

Others assume that the customer has all the information
needed to make a buying decision, and consequently don't
check for understanding.

If you assume that a sale is not possible, the chances are
that the customer will assume the same. Equally, the reverse
is true. There are some assumptions, however, that you should
go in with:

- Today *is* the day.
- You *do* offer the best value for the money.
- You *do* stand by everything you say.

If you demonstrate your complete belief in everything
that you are saying, the customer will believe you. Inexperi-
enced salespeople sometimes appear surprised when the customer says "Yes." This is because they assumed they would
get a "No." It should be the other way around, and once it is,
the whole emphasis of the meeting will alter.

Getting to the Right Person

To ensure that you are talking to the right person, research is
vital. There is nothing worse than ending a long presentation
only to hear:

"I'll talk to my boss."

Or:

"I'll bring it up at the next budget meeting."

Or:

"The person you should be talking to is out of town at the moment, but if you would like to come back in a week or so…"

The first thing to do is identify the MAN. This is all about researching the customer's ability to say "Yes."

M Money: Can they afford the product?

A Authority: Can this person authorize the purchase?

N Need: Do they need or want the product?

If you identify the MAN early in the sales call, your chances of successfully closing increase dramatically. The best way to identify the MAN is simply to ask:

"So that I don't waste any of your time, are you the right person to talk to for this sort of decision?"

You can do this at the first visit, but be careful, because customers might lie, not wanting to admit that they are not in authority. So you must give their egos room to breathe. Try putting it another way:

"Is there anyone else you would like to involve in our discussions?"

Or:

"Is there anybody else you would like me to invite to the demonstration we are going to do for you?"

Or:

"Should I send a copy of the numbers to anybody else?"

As a general rule, always try to involve the boss.

On the road to closing a sale you will come across various people who will influence your success.

The Decision Influencers

These are the people who make recommendations but do not actually make the final decisions. They have to be courted. They have to be convinced the product will benefit themselves and their departments and they have to be given a reason to lobby on your behalf. They are susceptible to flattery and should be told how important they are to the decision and how much their input counts.

The Decision Maker

The decision maker is probably the decision influencer's boss and is, as the name suggests, the one who makes the decisions. If you can get to this person directly, then go for it. Don't, however, ignore the influencers. If you need to come back with another proposition, you want the influencers on your side, rather than feeling antagonistic towards you, and possibly blocking your way to the decision maker. If they feel you have slighted them, they will take every opportunity to bad-mouth your product or service once it is installed and will ensure that you get no repeat orders. If the influencer agrees to recommend your solution but the decision maker is unavailable, you need to use the *Subject to Close*. For example:

"I understand that Mr. Smith isn't available today, but just to clarify it in my mind, if we get his approval, are you ready to proceed?"

When Mr. Smith returns the following week, you can use this agreement to pre-close the sale:

"While tying up loose ends with your colleague last week, he said that, subject to your final approval, he was pleased with the situation."

In this way you have made the influencer commit himself. He will lose face if he consequently fails to get the solution accepted and you have an impressive third-party reference to use in the meeting with the boss.

Decision-Making Unit

Purchasing responsibility that is spread over several departments, or that involves a number of different people is known as a decision-making unit. In this case, you must find out exactly how the unit is constructed. Who has responsibility for which part? Who reports to whom? How does the unit fit within the company as a whole? Does one member have the final decision or veto? What time frames and communication methods are used?

To answer these questions you will have to instigate some detailed research and undertake some perceptive questioning. This is not easy, but it is very necessary.

The rest of this chapter is a summary of rules and techniques that will help you bring your customer to the state of being ready to buy.

Ensure Complete Understanding

Never try to baffle prospective customers with technical jargon, or any language that they won't understand. They probably won't be impressed, and they certainly won't make a buying decision unless they are sure they have fully grasped what you are saying.

They may not want to admit that they don't understand, so it is up to you to check that they do. If they don't fully understand the proposal and don't want to admit it, they will not close. They will say something along the lines of:

"All right, leave me some literature and I'll give you a call."

Remember, you can't close until the prospective customer *completely understands* your proposal, so check understanding at each stage.

If You Don't Close, You Are Working for the Competition

You can do all the preliminary work of identifying prospective customers, approaching them, alerting them to their problems, and explaining ways in which these can be solved. But if you fail to close the sale, you have only set that customer up to buy from the next person who comes asking for the order: your competitor.

Structured Training's Steps of the Sale

Closing must be a pre-planned part of the overall sale, an end that you are working methodically towards right from the first moment of contact.

To make a sale, you must create a need to buy within the prospective customer that equals your own need to sell. That

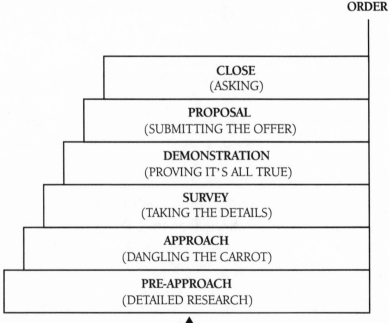

ORDER

CLOSE
(ASKING)

PROPOSAL
(SUBMITTING THE OFFER)

DEMONSTRATION
(PROVING IT'S ALL TRUE)

SURVEY
(TAKING THE DETAILS)

APPROACH
(DANGLING THE CARROT)

PRE-APPROACH
(DETAILED RESEARCH)

▲
PROSPECTING
(FINDING NEW CUSTOMERS)

can be achieved in stages throughout the sales process. By breaking the process down into stages, you can identify each stage's objectives and ensure that they are achieved before moving on. You can also measure your performance by generating success ratios for each stage and comparing one month or one quarter with the next, to ensure that your performance is consistently improving.

The Japanese Way

One Japanese computer company (FACOM) produces a sales checklist that has made them a winner in every market they tackle. Called "Profile of a Sale," it lists the eleven key stages a salesperson is required to go through, from the beginning to the end of a potential sale. (See p. 48.)

Aim to Achieve a Win-Win Situation

A win-win situation means that the seller wins by selling and the buyer wins by buying. If you give your customer room to win, then he or she will buy from you again. If a sale seems like a victory to the seller at the expense of the buyer, it is an unsatisfactory close, even though the sale was made.

If customers are unsure about making the final decision, it means that they are afraid of something. In most cases this is a fear caused by lack of knowledge. Customers need to be made brave enough to make the decision. That means they need to be reassured and helped over the fear of change.

Watch for the "Ready" Signals

Timing is vital in closing any sale. How do you decide the right moment to ask for the order? If you get the timing right, your chances of receiving a positive response increase by over 50 percent.

Profile of a Sale

1. RESEARCH PROSPECTIVE CUSTOMER
   Annual report. Company structure. Management.

2. ESTABLISH CONTACTS
   Plan objectives for each call. Top down or bottom up?

3. MEET DECISION MAKER AND RECOMMENDER

4. ESTABLISH NEEDS AND WANTS WITH DECISION MAKER
   Probe for company five-year plans with decision maker.
   What are the company's key business decisions?
   Who makes these decisions?

5. BASIS OF DECISION
   Unique to FACOM?
   Relevant to decision maker. Written down?
   Can FACOM satisfy all points?
   Favorable cost/benefit ratio?

6. FACOM REVIEW
   Review Basis of Decision with manager and assess
   percentage chance of obtaining the order.

7. RESOURCE ALLOCATION FOR SURVEY

8. SURVEY
   Review findings with customer's middle management.
   Have you established all objections?

9. PRESENTATION
   Plan and rehearse.

10. PROPOSAL
    Document only what you have sold.
    Does it satisfy all the points in the Basis of Decision?
    Sense of urgency?

11. CLOSE
    Close quickly or find out why not.
    Have you followed the Profile?

To help you decide on the right moment, look for "ready" signals. These are things buyers say or do that reveal they are ready. A typical verbal "ready" signal might be:

"Do you offer the system in other configurations?"

Physical, nonverbal "ready" signals might be harder to read, and require a reasonable knowledge of body language. Don't rely on just one body gesture but look for clusters of posture changes to demonstrate that the customer's resistance is disappearing and he or she is feeling relaxed and open towards you and your suggestions.

Imagine that you are selling to a customer who is seated behind his desk. You are painting pictures and emphasizing key points with your hands. You are trying to transmit your enthusiasm for your product to your customer. Such enthusiasm is infectious. (In fact, in selling there is only one thing more infectious and that is *lack* of enthusiasm.) The customer's fingers are pressed together at the tips, in a pyramid. This tells you that your proposals are being critically appraised but there are still some doubts. The customer is leaning back in his chair. If he were to change his position, stop pyramiding with his hands, and lean forward towards you, he would be indicating that his appraisal was finished and he was ready. If, on the other hand, his pyramiding were to change to folded arms across his chest and he remained leaning back in his chair, the body language signal would be negative. He would probably, but not definitely, have decided "No."

Imagine three different reactions of a senior executive listening to your sales presentation:

1. In the first reaction he is pyramiding again, which means critical appraisal.

2. A sure "ready" signal is when his fingers entwine and his hands comfortably clasp his lower stomach, arms at rest. He has decided.

3. Ask the right closing question and he will uncross his legs and lean forward. He is ready to buy.

Picture three stages of positive evaluation:

1. In the first, the customer, seated behind his desk, is doubtful. Her doubt is signified by the hand stroking her chin and by the arm defensively guarding her chest. She is leaning back.
2. As you talk, something hits a hot button. The customer stops stroking her chin. Her head tilts to one side, resting on a vertical finger and on the hand that was stroking her chin. She still leans back and she still presents the defensive arm barrier, but she is interested.
3. If you see that you have hit the hot button and run with it, the customer's interest may build. She may lean forward, chin still held in her hand, one elbow on the desk. Her defensive arm barrier drops to the surface of the desk. Go for it.

Now imagine a very uninterested, unresponsive junior decision influencer. He sees changes and that means more work for him if he goes along with your proposals. He is limp, with his legs crossed at the ankles, and his hands loosely clasped on his lap. There are no tangible defensive barriers, but anyone can see that he is negative.

How can you stimulate him into positive action? Perhaps help him see that by introducing a significant technological improvement for his company, the recognition he receives will outweigh the hassle of extra work. A hot button again, and this time we know the signal is green because the leg is crossed with the ankle of one leg resting on the knee of the other leg. The head tilts slightly to one side. The hands are still resting on the lap.

Continue to develop this hot button and the decision influencer will want more information to help him sell your proposals to his bosses. The leg comes down and his stance is wide open, receptive. He leans forward and his clasped hands move up and away from his body, almost begging.

A more aggressively negative decision influencer might have tightly folded arms, chin drawn in, legs stiff and ankles locked together. He is decidedly frosty. But hit a hot button and his chin will come up, his legs will pull back. He is more open but the ankles are still crossed, the arms still folded. Keep going and one arm will unfold and begin stroking his chin—a sure sign that he is interested. Stroking stops, head tilts to one side and he is ready to proceed. Go for it.

A senior executive in the final stages of deciding to buy eagerly leans forward. She stops stroking her chin and looks directly at you. Don't miss this one. She's waiting for you to ask for the order.

And for any salespeople who have come this far and still fear having to ask for the order—if you see the palms of your customer's hands rubbing up and down the tops of his knees and thighs, he is impatient and eager to buy. You should ask for the order quickly but confidently.

"Can we call it a deal?"

"Will you sign up with us?"

"Can I have your order today?"

"How many do you want to stock for the first month?"

If you *don't* ask, this guy will throw you out on your ear.

Build Yourself a Benefit Bank

Every salesperson should develop a benefit bank, covering all the reasons a customer should buy, cross-referenced with the competition's benefits. It is vital to have a list of reasons why the customer should buy from you.

You should be able to present the features and their resulting benefits in an easy, clear way. You should also be able to demonstrate that your product or service is unique in some way or that it has a strong advantage that customers will not get from other suppliers. Once you have the benefits sorted out, then you just have to learn the best way to present them.

Remember, research has shown that there are five presentation words that really turn customers on. When they are used customers will sit up and listen. Customers will also remember these words after you have left.

- **Increase**
- **Improve**
- **Reduce**
- **Save**
- **Gain**

Try to use all five, linking them into your benefit bank.

If you plan it right, you will find you are closing to the right person at the right time on the right product or service. If you use the win-win formula, you will find that the sales process gathers its own momentum, carrying itself through to a natural close. By making sure that the customer is "ready" to be closed, the closing itself is almost a formality.

6

Benefit Bank Development, Proofs, and Selling Tools*

For sales managers, vice presidents, and directors of sales only. Salespeople should move directly to Chapter 7.

I want to ask all the sales managers, vice presidents of sales, and directors of sales who are reading this book some serious questions. Do you give your salespeople the training and the tools they need to maximize their opportunities to close? Do you help them develop their benefit banks? Do you regularly update and refresh the data in those banks and test your salespeople on their competence in using the benefit bank?

Have you provided specific tools for converting negative responses into a positive response? For example, customers say, "Looks good. Send me a quote." Is this serious or is it a put-off? Why do they want a quote? Do they need to sell the proposal to someone else who has the power to make the decision? Are they saying "Send me a quote" because they haven't got the guts to say what they really want to say, which is, "No. Go away and leave me alone"?

The benefit bank, the proofs, the selling tools, should all be dedicated to changing this very common "Looks good. Send me a quote" into *"Looks great. When can we have it?"*

And for the staller who says, "I need to wait for a few more quotes," the benefit bank, the proofs, and the tools need to be dedicated to turning this into, *"This looks like the best deal I'm going to get."*

And for that old, everyday chestnut "I'll think about it," the benefit bank, the proofs, and the tools need to be dedicated to achieving the response, *"Let's do it right away."*

Without your help, very few of your salespeople will do anything about this on their own. Without your help, probably 75 percent of their closing opportunities will go down the drain. You're paid to do something about this, so *do* it.

Start with the most powerful selling tools there are, and the easiest ones for you to acquire: letters from satisfied customers, third-party references, and written referrals.

How many such letters are buried in the files, forgotten and never used? Dig them out. Send copies (at least ten of each) to *every* salesperson. Provide display albums so that they can use them professionally. Add at least six customer letters to every proposal and quotation you send out.

How many customer letters are in your salespeople's files, jealously guarded, for their eyes only? Who do they think they're in competition with? Their own colleagues? Their own company? Get hold of those letters and circulate them to every salesperson.

A third-party reference letter doesn't have to be written directly to the person using it to be effective proof. *Any* letter to *any* person in your company that says "We are very pleased with the service and would recommend it to anyone" is the most powerful closing tool you can get.

Set your salespeople a target and make things happen. Each salesperson *must* secure one new customer letter each month. No excuses. After six months you will have enough good letters to build them into a special brochure—*What the Customers Say*—about your business. Produce a new brochure every six months, containing all the new letters, and in two years you will have eclipsed your competitors with this alone.

7

Overcoming Price Conditioning

Many salespeople seem to be obsessed with price, much more so than most customers. Their obsession usually comes out in the form of offering discounts, which can become a drug to some salespeople. Just like drugs, discounts can screw you up.

If you offer a 5 percent discount this time, customers will ask for more next time, and you will have a hard time talking them out of it.

Prospective customers need to be conditioned about price. They are price sensitive only as a result of the actions of the sales profession.

People use price to indicate the value of the product. If you are thinking of spending a weekend away at a hotel but know nothing about the place, you would use the room price as an indication of the value of the product. If a used-car salesman welcomes you on to the lot with the announcement that this car "has $400 off the sticker price this week," you immediately know that he wants to sell you the car more than you want to buy it. If he is willing to give you that much off, then the chances are that you will ask for a bit more. You have been negatively price conditioned. If, however, he works at selling the perfect vehicle to you, asking you questions about your needs and stimulating your interest and desire to buy, only talking about price at the end, you are then in a more positive frame of mind towards both him and the car. You have been positively price conditioned.

If customers say, "It's too expensive," never argue with them and never agree with them by offering to make a concession. Just ask, "Relative to what?" Establish the facts they are working with. Are they comparing it to the last time they bought this particular product or service? Are they comparing it to something completely different? Are they comparing it to their available budget or to the prices of the competition or to something they heard from their colleagues?

Keep price conditioning in mind all the time you are listening and talking. Prepare customers for the fact that if they want the best solution to their problem, they must expect to pay for it.

Never Knock the Competition

Never run down the competitor's products, but make sure that you know more about them than your customers do. Otherwise your customers could be running rings around you.

If your customers tell you that a competitor's price is 10 percent lower than yours but they will do business with you if you can match it, they are telling you something very important. They are saying that they would prefer to buy from you. If they wanted to deal with the competition, they would want you to undercut in order to justify the risk. If they can buy it cheaper, why are they discussing it with you at all? Perhaps the competition can't make the delivery on time or produce sufficient quantities.

These customers have already agreed that they need the product. You now only have to "sell" them on the extra 10 percent cost—not a difficult task compared to selling the whole 100 percent of the product. If they claim that yours is a more expensive product, you must know why that is. Is it because it is more reliable? Does it last longer? Is it made better? Is it easier to use? If they continue to dwell on the cost, try asking them if they always buy on price. If the answer is "Yes," then ask what sorts of cars they drive. If they admit to driving bare-bones economy cars, then you are probably talking to the wrong people, but the chances are that they drive cars that are a bit more expensive because of their comfort, power, reliability, service back-up, or whatever.

Justify the Difference

People will always pay more for something if they feel they are getting more for their money, but they won't pay more for an identical product. If customers ask you how much discount you are willing to give, don't answer and don't haggle. Remember that, in the long term, the more you discount the harder it becomes to sell. If customers say they want a discount, never reply by asking how much they are looking for. You would be giving them a license to knock you down.

The Right Way to Close on a Discount

If customers do ask for a discount, check that they are ready to make a buying decision then and there if the price can be agreed. If you can't do a deal today, don't give a discount. Otherwise they will use your price to shop around. Never give a discount to someone who isn't going to buy from you.

Don't feel you have to discount in huge jumps. Keep an open mind, but don't haggle like a market trader. That would devalue you and your product.

If customers say they can do the deal today, then turn it into a trade, not a gift. If you give a 10 percent discount, will they pay cash on delivery? If you give a discount, will they buy a greater volume? If they agree to changes in the after-sales package, then perhaps you can drop the price. If they agree to a longer contract of commitment, then perhaps you can make a concession on the price.

Educate customers to realize that if they want something, they will have to give something. That way you are not devaluing the product.

The Added-Value Close

You can charge higher prices only if you are giving added value, but you have to make sure customers understand that.

Explain all the things that they will gain by buying from you. You have to demonstrate all the benefits the higher price includes. You need to be brave enough to look customers in the eye and say:

"Part of what you get for this price is me."

Then look at the minus side, and give examples of what would be taken away if they decide to buy something cheaper. Make some calculations, such as dividing the cost by the life span of the product. Rather than talking about a cost of $2,000, talk about $20 per week for the next two years. Then multiply the savings and gains that your product will offer, making the figure as high as possible. You want to make the costs look smaller and the savings look bigger.

You need to have all these numbers at your fingertips before you go in for the close, but your close will look more effective if you actually work them out in front of the customers, as if for the first time. If they agree to the calculations as you go along, they will have to agree with the conclusion.

By adding value to the package, you minimize your own "price fight" and weaken customers' price resistance.

The Suicide Close

This is a true story.

A replacement-window salesman called on a customer who was haggling about the price and driving a hard bargain. They talked for a while and finally the salesman said, "OK, I'm not actually the salesman who should be servicing this area, I'm the sales manager. The reason I'm here is that the salesman committed suicide yesterday." The customer, taken aback by this novel form of closing, offered his condolences and then asked what this had to do with him. "Well," said the sales manager, "because I don't have to pay the salesman his commission on the sale, I can offer it to you as a discount."

The customer, who was one of Structured Training's course directors, laughed and said, "That's the first time I've heard of the Suicide Close." The sales manager thought for a moment and nodded. "Right on. It's a cracker, ain't it!"

The customer did not buy.

The John Ruskin Close

Early on in the sale, ask customers if you can establish whether they believe in buying on price or on value for money. They will almost certainly go for value. Later on in the meeting take a business card out of your pocket with a quote from John Ruskin (1819-1900) on the back and point out that it is over 150 years old. Either give it to the customer or offer to read it out loud:

"It is unwise to pay too much, but it is unwise to pay too little. When you pay too much you lose a little money and that is all, but when you pay too little you sometimes lose everything, because the thing that you've bought isn't capable of doing the thing which it was bought to do.

The common law of business balance prohibits you from paying a little and receiving a lot—it can't be done. If you deal with the lowest bidder it would be as well to add something for the risk you run, and if you can do that you can afford to buy something better."

Lawful Prey

Ruskin penned an even more powerful potential Price Close:

"There is hardly anything in the world today that some man cannot make just a little worse and sell just a little cheaper, and the people who buy on price alone are this man's lawful prey."

At Structured Training I encountered many sales managers who still thought training at rock-bottom prices was the best money could buy. I used the Ruskin quotation on the back of my business cards and I never encountered a single person who was happy at the thought of being somebody else's lawful prey.

Don't State It, Sell It

When customers ask how much the product costs, remember that you are a salesperson. Don't simply say, "$2,000 plus tax and shipping, etc." Instead, tell them everything they are going to get for the price. Do all the arithmetic—the adding, subtracting, multiplying, and dividing—that we talked about earlier in this chapter. In this way customers will end up being positively price conditioned.

8

Closing With a Clipboard

Every salesperson needs a decent-sized, quality clipboard in order to close a sale. You simply can't close effectively with a little pocketbook. You need something professional-looking on which to make your notes, draw your diagrams, and keep your benefit lists for instant access.

When you first meet prospective customers, you should begin by exchanging business cards. If your customers don't have cards, that might sound a warning bell at the back of your mind. Could it be that they aren't decision makers at all? If they do have cards to give you, then you should clip them to the board in front of you, so that you never forget their names and so that you use their names more often.

Before you start, ask their permission to take notes. They are unlikely to say "No" and will be impressed by your professionalism.

Plan the contents of your clipboard to make sure you get everything right. It should have checklists of all the questions you need to ask as well as the benefits that you should be getting across, plus any facts, numbers, or third-party reference letters that you may need as part of your sales pitch.

The Order-Form Close

We have already covered this close in some detail in Chapter 4. Sixty-four percent of all salespeople who sell to retail organizations prefer it, and it is vital that a clipboard is used throughout.

The Criteria-for-Ordering Close

The Criteria-for-Ordering (CFO) Close is the industrial equivalent of the Order-Form Close. Just like its retail counterpart, it starts at the very beginning of the sale and runs through to the very end. It forms the basis of the entire presentation and proposal.

Inside your clipboard you should have a pre-printed list of all the major plus points for the product or service and for yourself as a supplier. A second list specifies what each plus point means for your customer and for you (see the sample CFO on p. 69). So you say to the customer, "Which of these criteria are important to you?"

If the list has been well thought out, the customer will answer, "All of them," and by the time you get to the bottom of the list you will have large check marks next to each relevant plus point. You then know exactly in which direction to gear your sales presentation. Everything you have to do, to prove and to demonstrate, is on the list, and you will have prepared every answer.

Once it is all done, the list is still there in your clipboard and you are able to refer to it as you move in for the close.

"Have we satisfied your criteria for ordering on all the points I've marked?" you ask innocently.

"Um...yyess...I think so."

"Fine. Can you give me an order number, then, so that we can get moving on this?"

The Ben Franklin Balance Sheet

When you are up against strong competition, the CFO Close becomes an advanced form of the Ben Franklin Balance Sheet. In its simple form this involves taking a plain sheet of paper, drawing a vertical line down the center and writing two headings—"for" and "against"—at the top of each column.

This is a great method for helping poor decision makers to reach a decision. The "for" list, with your able assistance, should be three times as long as the "against" list.

What criteria for ordering does this customer use?

Plus points	Customer's Criteria
PRICE	Best value for money.
DELIVERY	Keeping promises, or being able to help you out because you've waited until the last minute before placing the order.
QUALITY	Meets your specifications—and KEEPS meeting them with no defects.
SERVICE RESPONSE	Quick and effective—no delays to cost you money in lost production.
COMPETENCE	Our service, warehouse, and accounting people get your orders right, sort out the paperwork right, and handle returns without hassle or delay.
RELIABILITY	Of the product. Documented record of performance that proves longer life.
RUNNING COSTS	As low as possible.
MAINTENANCE COSTS	As low as possible.
PERFORMANCE	Maximum possible on a consistent basis.
SAFETY	Meets all the current and known future regulations—also will be acceptable to your work force.
COMMUNICATIONS	Easy to do business with. Easy to get hold of the people you want to talk to.
PHILOSOPHY	The company puts the customer first, not its own problems.

When it's a case of customers being unable to make up their minds between one supplier and another, the columns on your clipboard sheet should be headed with the names of the suppliers under consideration.

Your company's name should always be on the far left.

If you have a CFO list, *your* column should already be completed. Take it out from under the clip in your clipboard and slip it into a clear plastic pocket on the inside cover, so it's on the far left when your clipboard is open.

Your competitors get all the right-hand sheet space, but with your CFO list on their left, how can they win? You never, never knock your competition; just point out the differences.

And by the way, you always start with your list and never with the competition's, just in case customers are called away in the middle of your presentation. Imagine leaving them with a list of your competition's plus points only–and in your handwriting.

You can win in two ways. You highlight the plus points of your deal, which are over and above what the competition is offering according to the lists in your clipboard. You can also use these plus points to justify any price difference that is not in your favor. You then apply the "options lost" technique, and go through your competitor's lists, highlighting what customers won't get if they buy from them.

"Well, it looks pretty obvious, doesn't it?" you conclude, and then close.

The Options-Lost Close

The Options-Lost Close is also a powerful tool when you're faced with customers who are telling you they're going to wait a while and think about it–and you know they're going to throw away a chunk of money if they do that.

You simply have to write down on your closing clipboard a list of the options they will lose if they don't buy now. Things like the following:

- The special December campaign discount.
- The price which goes up 8 percent on January 1st.
- Delivery before Christmas.
- The loss of benefit for the month they're thinking it over.

The longer you can make this list the better. Then you add up all the items, having quantified them all in money terms, and you have a lump sum written down that customers can clearly see is the cost of their delaying the decision.

"That's quite a waste of good money while you are worrying for a month or two," you point out. "Wouldn't you rather not have the worry?"

The Wedding-Cake Close

This is a natural follow-up to a comparison of your check list with an established supplier's. You've already proven that you have the edge and can provide a better all-around quality deal, but you still have to fight against years of entrenched habit.

"It would be unreasonable of me to expect you to give me all your widget business, and for you to discard Johnson after all these years," you say. "It would be like a guest at a wedding reception eating the whole wedding cake. I'm not greedy. But how about giving us a slice of the wedding cake—say, 20 percent of your widget business? That way you keep Johnson happy, you try us out, and, with two suppliers, you have second-source insurance, keeping both of us on our toes in the right kind of competitive spirit. You can't lose."

And as you speak, you draw the wedding cake on your clipboard pad, with a small slice cut out of it. But practice first. Drawing cakes is not everyone's talent!

If the customer buys, then of course you go for a bit more of the business each time you call back. An increase of 20 percent to 50 percent is an easy jump to make, unless you let someone down.

The Calendar Close

Instead of a clipboard use your calendar. It could be a pocket calendar, but a handsome desk one will be much more effective and easier to use.

Get into the habit of carrying the calendar with you in every selling situation. At the end of the sale, when you have covered everything except when the customer is going to get delivery, you get out the calendar as you close, open it at the next month and say:

"Now, I want to be available when the unit is delivered. I always like to make sure personally that everyone is happy on the first day. When would you like delivery? What's your most convenient date and time?"

Most customers will say, "I'm not in a big rush."

"Okay," you say. "How does Tuesday, December 15 at 10:15 in the morning sound?"

"Sounds okay."

"Great."

You shut your calendar, stand up, and extend your hand.

"It's a pleasure having you as a customer."

Signing-Up Techniques

If you are using an Order-Form Close, all you have to do is turn the clipboard around, extend it towards the customer with a pen and say:

"Will you just okay this for me? Here at the bottom."

With other sorts of closes, you finish off with the One-Two Close:

1. Are you happy with everything?
2. Can we go ahead, then?

Once you have asked these two questions you really do have to shut up and endure the pressure of your own silence— for at least five seconds, and preferably more if the response is slow in coming.

X Marks the Spot

This signing technique is useful in any kind of selling where you use an order form or credit finance document.

You fill the form out and then you put a penciled X where the customer has to sign. You then hand the customer the form in your clipboard, which still has the "criteria for ordering" list clearly visible on the left-hand side. You don't need to say anything!

As soon as the form is in front of the customer, get up and check a measurement or something similar (go to the rest room, perhaps). When you return, if the form still isn't signed, offer your pen. If you can bear it, still don't say anything. Words might let the customer off the hook.

The Objectives Checklist

A particularly effective checklist is one that covers the customer's objectives. (See example on p.75.)

The salesperson can actually use the list to broaden the mind of the prospective customer, opening up a whole new world of possible cost savings and productivity increases.

The list should be produced and explained at an appropriately early stage in the presentation.

"Our products usually enable our customers to achieve seven objectives that are pretty important to them. Most of these involve saving money. I've got the objectives listed on this sheet. Can I run through them and ask which of them are relevant to your situation?"

The salesperson runs through the list of objectives with the customer, who will almost certainly be actively worried about some of the items, though others might not have seemed relevant before. In most cases customers will agree that they want to achieve all seven of the objectives; they never want less than four of them.

Once their objectives have been identified, the salesperson goes on to define more precisely what the customer wants to achieve for each section. The precise objectives are written in the spaces provided under each heading.

The seller then asks the prospective customer to put the objectives in order of importance. After this the rest of the call and the justification for the purchase should be smooth sailing. The completed Objectives sheet becomes the first page of any resultant proposal.

OBJECTIVES

Customer _____

Date _____

What does the customer want to do – and why does he/she want to do it?

Detailed objectives that this customer wants to achieve (Strike out the sections that do not apply)	Order of Priority
INCREASE PRODUCTION	
REDUCE HANDLING TIME	
REDUCE LABOR REQUIREMENT	
REDUCE MAINTENANCE COSTS	
BETTER UTILIZATION OF EQUIPMENT	
BETTER UTILIZATION OF SPACE	
IMPROVE LABOR RELATIONS/SAFETY (Union attitude, accident rate, absenteeism, fatigue)	
OTHER FACTORS	

9

Building Checklists for the Closing Clipboard*

For sales managers, vice presidents, and directors of sales only. Salespeople should move directly to Chapter 10.

I f you want to significantly increase your business, you should provide your salespeople with the proper tools as well as the skills to use them. The following checklist suggests a possible plan of action using some of the tools and techniques you've learned in this book.

☐ Provide each of your salespeople with a good-quality, legal-size, professional-looking clipboard.

☐ Call a meeting of the entire sales team and get everyone's input into building a Criteria-for-Ordering list for each of your products or services and your customer's Objectives lists.

☐ Practice using the lists with your salespeople.

☐ Test their knowledge of your competitors.

☐ Make sure they each carry a large page-a-day calendar.

☐ Make sure they can each draw wedding cakes.

10

Closing Over
the Telephone

Most salespeople seem to be terrified of the telephone, but it is in fact their greatest asset. It is one of the most powerful marketing tools available too, but only if you choose to use it effectively.

More excuses are given for failing to attain objectives using the telephone than in any other area of selling, whether it be appointment making, order taking, or closing. Everyone sees the problems involved with the telephone but never the opportunities. It is vital to study your telephone technique in detail, then maximize the strengths and minimize the weaknesses.

Some salespeople seem to forget the objective of their call and simply end up having a nice friendly chat with their customers, with no positive outcome. This may be very pleasant, but it is not selling. Others attack every phone call in a high-pressure, results-oriented manner. They ignore the important aspect of selling themselves and don't think about the emotional impact of their voice on the customer. The result is that customers don't like what they are hearing and immediately put up barriers.

In between these two extremes is a successful balance of tangible and intangible elements.

The Twin-Track Approach

This can be one of the most effective tele-selling methods. It makes use of two tracks, the tangible and the intangible, to plan and execute calls.

The Intangible Track

1. Make sure you approach the telephone with a positive "Yes, I can" attitude, because it will come across in your voice, and you will infect the listener with your confidence and enthusiasm.

2. Smile before you pick up the phone. It may sound corny, but it will make a difference to your voice. When the corners of your mouth turn up, your voice sounds happy.

3. Take advantage of every opportunity to sell yourself and your company.

4. Try to go all out for each customer, rather than doing as little as you can get away with. That doesn't just mean going all out for the ones who shout the loudest.

5. Make sure that you never over-promise or under-deliver. Promises are like babies: they are fun to make, but sometimes very difficult to deliver.

6. Make sure you always sound polite, helpful, and caring. Try listening to a recording of yourself to make sure you sound as you think you do. Putting personality and projection into your voice takes constant practice.

7. Remain alert to customers' moods and tones of voice, and then respond accordingly. Listening is a conscious mental process, whereas hearing is just a physical act.

8. Empathize with customers' concerns and needs, which means seeing their viewpoints without necessarily agreeing with them.

9. Always accept complaints as opportunities to improve your service, never as problems.

10. Ask yourself when a customer last said, "Thanks for your help and advice." It should be happening all the time.

The Tangible Track

1. Define your objective, whether it is appointment making, research, or making a final close. If you can't achieve your main objective, what is your fall-back objective?

2. Always have all the relevant paperwork, records, and your calendar on hand when you call.

3. Make sure you have an effective and flexible script, with all your key points ready.

4. Develop an effective attention getter to open up the conversation.

5. Prepare your key questions and make sure they are open and not closed. "Yes" and "No" answers over the phone are worse than useless.

6. Make sure you have your benefit bank complete and on hand. You are more likely to get an appointment if you talk benefits rather than features.

7. Listen for "ready" signals, and be prepared to use a trial close the moment you hear one.

8. Prepare answers to the objections that are likely to arise.

9. Promise yourself that you will attempt to close every call to the *highest* objective.

10. Keep a record of calls converted to completed objectives, and check that your ratio is improving on a steady curve.

A recent analysis showed that 74 percent of successful tele-closers use the Alternative Choice Close, just as in face-to-face selling.

When talking to the switchboard operator you can ask:

"Would you be able to help me with some information that I need or would you prefer to pass me on to someone who can?"

With a secretary:

"Would it be possible for me to talk to Mr. Jones now or would it be better if I called back later this afternoon?"

With a customer:

"If today is inconvenient how about if I come in to see you next Tuesday? Would the morning or the afternoon be better?"

If you offer customers a choice, they are likely to make one rather than simply say "No." By rejecting one of the alternatives they are, by inference, accepting the other.

Trial Closing

When you get a "ready" signal, you can use a trial close. It is much harder to spot the signals when you aren't face to face, but it can help to ask questions.

"Do you need delivery by the end of the month?"

And then listen. If the answer is, "Yes, it is very important that we have it by then," it is time to close.

If you can tell that the customer is imagining owning the product, then you are practically there.

Customers will also use "If we..." phrases on the phone.

"If we decide to go with you, could you install it for us?"

Don't just answer "Yes." Ask another question back:

"Absolutely no problem. When would you like us to do the installation?"

Be aware of changes in tone of voice. A laugh or chuckle suggests the customer is imagining owning the product.

The worst thing customers can say to you is, "I'm not quite ready yet." However, if you are prepared to answer customer objections, you can ask what points are still worrying them and go through things once more.

Selling Across

Always help customers obtain a complete package. If they are buying a product from you that needs something else to go with it (such as sand with cement, nails with a hammer), make sure that you can offer it to them somehow.

This is another way to use the twin-track approach. The telephone is an ideal method of adding on another product once the first sale has been made. Customers actually enjoy being sold across, because once they have made the first decision to purchase, they are impatient to get the final result. If they have been sold cement it is because they want to see the wall built at the bottom of their garden. So they will be keen to buy the bricks and sand, and to purchase a cement mixer and whatever other tools they need. And there is nothing as frustrating as buying a new toy for the children, taking it home and unwrapping it, only to find that there are no batteries. Why didn't they sell me some batteries?

Selling Up

This means increasing the value of the sale and, again, customers enjoy the experience. They will be very frustrated if they buy the first product you suggest, only to find a few months later that there is something else on the market that is marginally more expensive but does a great deal more for them.

But, if you are going to add value to the sale by moving the customer to a product further up the market, don't do it simply to make a bit more money because that does not create a win-win situation.

Closing on a Complaint

Angry customers are like balloons full of hot air. They are in a very volatile, potentially explosive state.

You could argue with them and concentrate on winning the argument rather than the sale. This is like sticking a pin in the balloon: you will find that you end up with no balloon and hence no customer.

You could abdicate responsibility, saying that it's not your problem, which is tantamount to just letting go. The air would come rushing out, but you would have no idea where the balloon could go. It might end up in your manager's office, with the competition, or on a consumer watchdog program.

As long as the balloon is still inflated there is a chance that the situation can be saved. The best way is to hold on firmly to the balloon, which means taking responsibility and letting the air out gradually, in a controlled way. This means listening to the complaint for as long as the customer wants to talk about it.

Whoever answers the telephone must take possession of the complaint. If it is you, from the moment you answer it is your problem. You own it. Once you have asked questions and empathized with the customer, the air will go out of the balloon. You then say, "This is what I propose to do about the problem." If the customer says, "Yes, I agree," then you have solved the problem and the sale can be saved. If the customer says, "No," then you have to do some more questioning and some more listening because there is still some air in the balloon. When have all the facts, you can start making suggestions:

"So that will sort out this month's delivery for you, Mr. Jones, and to make sure the same thing doesn't happen again, should we increase the amount of next month's delivery by 10 percent? Should I just add it to the invoice, or would you prefer a separate one?"

If you pick your moment, you can close very successfully on a complaint. If you solve problems for customers you will be cementing relationships, and they will come back to you again the next time they have problems.

"Following Up Quotation" Closes

First, it is better to send proposals than just quotations.

Don't call up saying, "Have you received our quote?" You are merely asking for a negative reply. Instead, try saying, "Last

"Last week we sent you our proposals for increasing/improving/reducing/saving/gaining..."

Don't say, "Have you had a chance to look it over?" Try, "Can you give me the go-ahead? We're ready at this end."

If customers say that they have a few queries or points they're not happy with, don't say, "Oh, what are they?" That will get you into objection handling by telephone. Instead, say, "Okay, I'll be back in your area next week. I'll come over and go through them with you. Which day is most convenient for you, Monday or Tuesday?"

Exploding the Myth

There is a piece of "perceived wisdom" that says it is impossible to get big decisions over the phone. Most salespeople and managers believe that it can't be done. But it can, if you believe it can. Adopt a "Yes, I can" attitude.

An eighteen-year-old salesperson, fresh out of one of Structured Training's "Selling by Telephone" courses, proved this by closing an order for over $2 million over the telephone. She has subsequently closed many more deals this way, perhaps because she has been trained to know that it is possible.

Remember the bumblebee?

11

Classic Closes

H ere is a mixed bag of the real-life classic closes that have, over the years, served to make their users rich. They can be adapted and used by anyone who has the determination and open-mindedness to be really successful in this great profession called selling.

When Is an Order Really Lost?

This is about an order that was won after the customer had placed the same order with a competitor and paid a deposit of $2,600. The product was an expensive piece of metal finishing machinery.

Our hero, the salesperson who found that he had lost the order to a competitor, reported this calamity to his sales manager. The sales manager said, "Hold on a minute. We've got one of these in stock. We could deliver it to them tomorrow. What delivery is the competition offering?"

"Six weeks minimum," replied the salesperson.

"So all is not lost," said the sales director. "Come on, let's go and talk to the customer."

So they sat down with the customer and worked out the figures, which showed that by saving the six weeks' delay on delivery they could save the customer three times the $2,600 he had paid as a deposit. The manager who had actually placed the order was reluctant to let down the company with whom he had made the deal, and didn't believe that his boss would allow it. So they went to see the customer's boss and laid all the figures out in front of him. He was also doubtful about doing this to the competing supplier, so the sales manager offered an additional discount of $2,600 over the first year on the chips that went into the machine, and the deal was done.

So when is an order really lost? Never!

As an extra bonus, the competition made such a song and dance about losing the deal that the customer ended up banning them from his premises forever.

The "Price Is Higher" Close

This is for salespeople with guts and tremendous willpower. They also need to have a top-quality product or service.

It begins when the customer says to you, "Your price is higher than the other people I've been talking to." You nod, say seriously, "*Yes*, it is," and then shut up. After a few seconds the customer can't stand the silence and says, "I suppose you'll say that's because yours is better?" And you nod again, say seriously, "Yes, it is," and shut up again.

After a few seconds of this, most customers will sigh, say, "Okay, then" and buy.

The "Phone the Boss" Close

This is sometimes called the *Executive Cooperation Close.*

This time you are dealing with a final objection. You *know* it's a final objection because you've already asked, "Is this the only thing that's standing in the way of us doing business?"

It's only a point on price or delivery that is holding things up, with the customer wanting delivery two days sooner or digging his toes in for an additional discount. You can't make these sorts of decisions, so you ask the customer if you can use the phone to call your boss. The customer, of course, says, "Sure, go ahead."

You call your boss, explain the problem, and give the impression that you are having a hard time defending the customer's position. The boss gives in, apparently reluctantly.

You look at the customer, with the phone still to your ear, and say, "My boss says he'll do it, but only if I can give him an order now. Is that okay?"

Very rarely indeed is it not okay. So you tell your boss to go ahead and deliver, and the customer is impressed that you have pulled out all the stops for him.

The Coffee Pot Close

Some upscale retail outlets use this close effectively when customers are on the premises.

When customers come in, offer them coffee and make sure that it is so hot that they can't possibly start to drink it for ten minutes. They consequently have to sit there talking to you or look around the stock, and they become obligated to buy *something*. You have, after all, extended a gesture of friendship and hospitality towards them.

The same principle also works well on small, under-staffed trade show booths. One or two people can service a dozen prospective customers while they're waiting for their coffees to cool down to drinking temperature. It can even be a good idea to design the stand to look like a cafe, which will attract tired visitors to sit down for rest and refreshment.

Public Closes

This means giving a presentation to a group of people, who may not all be from the same company, and closing the whole group. If you can get one or two of them to say "Yes," the whole group will follow, rather like sheep.

I gave a demonstration of this technique live on television. There was only one chance to get this right. The customers were forty members of the Women's Guild, and the product was a computer-controlled dishwasher. It was more expensive than some of the competitors' products but very reliable. I used three pre-close stages to get to the real close, and all forty prospects said "Yes." It went as follows:

Pre-Close 1

"How do you feel about unemployment? I read somewhere the other day that we're losing 20,000 jobs a month in our manufacturing industries.

"Terrible. But I also read that if everyone in the country spent another $5.00 a week on domestic goods instead of foreign goods, this 20,000 jobs a month loss would turn into a 60,000 jobs a month gain. It's staggering to think it could be that easy, isn't it?'

Pre-Close 2

"How do you feel about washing dishes?" (Muttered replies like "horrible.") "How many hours a week do you spend doing it?" ("Too many.") "Twenty perhaps? What could you do with that time if you didn't have to waste it washing dishes? How many of you have a dishwasher?" (Only one.) "So all the rest of you do it the manual way."

Pre-Close 3

"When you go shopping, especially when you're looking for something for the home that has to last a long time, do you look for the cheapest price or the best value for money?" (Unanimous "best value.")

The Real Close

"I would like to demonstrate to you a new product that's a bit more expensive than others you could buy, but it's very, very good—and if you like what you see, I'd like to arrange to do another demonstration in each of your homes, to make sure you can live happily with a dishwasher. How do you feel about that?" (Unanimous "Yes.")

The Cocktail Party Close

This is a classic from the life insurance industry. If you tell a stranger at a cocktail party that you sell life insurance, the stranger disappears, almost like a puff of smoke. The words "I sell life insurance" can clear a room faster than shouting "Fire!" However, cocktail parties provide a source of potential customers. To increase prospects, try this subtle change in technique:

Stranger: "What do you do for a living?"

Insurance Agent: "I buy life insurance."

Stranger: *(Puzzled)* "What do you mean, you buy life insurance?"

Insurance Agent: "I buy life insurance for people at the lowest possible cost for the maximum possible benefits. Would you like me to buy you some?"

The Victor Hugo Close

This is another particularly good close for the insurance industry, using a quote from Victor Hugo: "Nothing, not even prison bars, can hold a man as securely as poverty in old age."

Like the John Ruskin Close discussed earlier, this is a great quote to have on the back of a business card, and can be adapted to fit most selling situations.

Any salesperson selling something that will increase the customer's profits can use the quote, just adding: "...and if your business doesn't increase its profits, you won't have much money to put into your pension fund, will you? Which, as you know, is the most tax-efficient thing a company owner can do with his money, Mr. Jones."

The Audio Cassette Close

This classic is about a salesperson who had submitted a proposal for a significant chunk of business to a customer he already knew reasonably well. But when he came to follow up the proposal and secure the order, he found that his customer was never there when he telephoned or called in person. It wasn't evasion. The guy really was terribly busy, with responsibilities for three factories, each one fifty or sixty miles from the other. He was spending 80 percent of his day in his car, and most of the other 20 percent in the factories. His secretary saw him only for about ten minutes a week.

The salesperson knew that the customer was a Frank Sinatra fan, as he was himself. So he unearthed a very old, very rare 78 record of Sinatra that he was sure the customer didn't have. He copied the track onto a cassette and sent it to the customer through the mail, with a cover letter.

A few days later, the customer was in his car, burning up the miles on the way to one of his factories and playing the tape. After a few minutes of Sinatra, the music faded and he heard the salesperson's voice.

"Hi, Mr. Arnold, I hope you like this tape. Sorry to interrupt, but I've been trying to speak to you for weeks now about our proposals for your chemicals supplies next quarter. If you don't have any questions, could you fax us the okay? Thanks. Enjoy the music." And the music faded back in again.

The customer was so taken with the originality of the close, he phoned his secretary when he got to his destination and told her to send the fax.

Closing a Closed Bid

There are, of course, many unethical ways to close a closed bid—what Wall Street might call insider trading and the law calls corruption. But there is also a perfectly ethical way of achieving the same end.

Most major closed-bid deals take weeks or even months to reach the bidding stage. During those weeks or months, the suppliers who are being considered have numerous meetings with the customer's people, to gather all the facts and figures so that they can present a meaningful bid. So this is what you do: after every meeting you send a report of the meeting's conclusions to every relevant customer contact. The report highlights the key benefits and cost savings that your deal will give the customer. By the time the bids are in, there should be a dozen or more such reports in the customer's files. All or most of them stand a good chance of being paper-clipped to your bid when it is examined. This is not a guarantee that you will win, but one company that has to give closed bids regularly wins more than 50 percent of the business it goes in for in this way—and at nowhere near the lowest price.

The "We've Got a Van in Your Area Tomorrow" Close

This is an absurdly simple classic that has enabled one company to boost its sales revenue by 20 percent in the first year that it started employing the close regularly.

Van deliveries are scheduled for the week ahead. The schedule is passed to someone in the sales office whose task it is to telephone every customer on the schedule the day before the scheduled delivery and say:

"You've got a delivery coming from us tomorrow. Is there anything else you'd like us to put on the van for you?"

Then that person pulls up the computerized records of all the other customers in the same town or on the route the delivery van will be taking and telephones them:

"We've got a van coming your way tomorrow. Is there anything we can put on it for you?"

It seems so obvious, doesn't it? But we know from experience that what this company is doing is exceptional. Too many companies have systems that are not flexible enough to allow for a fast turn-around, or else their sales offices think it would be too much trouble. Many simply haven't thought about it—or believe it is too simple to bother about. One company executive actually said to me:

"It's not very sophisticated, is it?"

But an increase of 20 percent in sales is a pretty sophisticated result.

12

Closing an Executive Committee

The conference room can be a battlefield for salespeople, and in order to win any battle you need confidence. But that is the one thing that can drain out of any salesperson when confronted by a high-powered committee of decision makers.

There are two battles going on in most of these situations, and neither of them is between the salesperson and the customers, because that sort of battle can lead only to a win-lose situation.

The first battle is happening within the salesperson's mind. When you lack confidence it means that there is a conflict going on inside your brain, the rational side fighting with the emotional side. That leads to an increased flow of adrenalin to keep the blood pumping around the body quickly, so that you can run away from the problem. Successful salespeople, however, can never run away, not if they want to close the sale. But that doesn't make them any less nervous.

To win the battle of the nerves, you have to face up truthfully to what you are feeling. If you tell yourself you are feeling "nervous" about the situation, you are actually using a euphemism for "scared." You must come to terms with how you feel and then you can deal with it. The way to achieve confidence is simply to know more about the subject than the people who sit around the conference table. If you are sure that you know more, your confidence will soar.

The second battle is between the committee members themselves. Whenever you have a team of ambitious, intelligent, opinionated people, you will have differences of opinion and conflicts of interest. Some executives will be interested in maintaining the status quo, while others will be intent on changing it. Some will want what you are proposing, while others will be dead set against it. Your proposals are a theater of war for these people.

This is the main problem most people face in an executive committee. To overcome this problem you need to know what is motivating everyone, and to understand some of the basics of human behavior and personality.

The Behavioral Mix

Everyone is made up of a unique behavioral mix. Personality characteristics are particularly noticeable around any conference table. Here are four examples:

The Customer With a Strong Need for Domination

Customers of this sort tend to be abrasive and defiant in their behavior. They may brag a lot and drop names more often than is necessary. They will try to monopolize any discussion and will be impatient with other people, interrupting them when they try to argue or introduce alternative points of view. They are argumentative and probably see no need for salespeople to exist at all. They will always claim to have all the answers.

A typical "Domination" manager once said that he didn't see why his company needed a sales force; he saw salespeople as being a "sore on the backside of industry."

How to Deal With "Domination" Customers

1. Never try to confront them. If you meet aggression with aggression you will just have conflict.
2. Control them passively by using open questions. Give the impression that they are controlling the meeting.
3. Give them plenty of back-up data because you will need to cross every "t" and dot every "i."
4. Let them drive the sale for you.
5. Let the other committee members shut them up.

The Customer With a Strong Need for Security

These people work on the premise that they had better keep their mouth shut so that their colleagues won't think they are stupid.

The stance here is silent and defensive. They will shrink back and say little, and will be very reluctant to come to a decision. They hate risk and want to maintain the status quo whenever possible. They are procrastinators and take a "that won't work" attitude toward everything.

One "Security" manager was heard agonizing over a decision and saying, "No, we made a wrong decision on something like this in 1958, and in 1964, and I'm not going to go through it again."

They were talking about buying a coffee machine.

How to Deal With "Security" Customers

1. Listen patiently and use open questions. You will need to watch their body language because they won't be saying much.
2. Do progress checks to ensure that you are talking on the same wavelength, and look for ways to become more tuned in to theirs.
3. Provide testimonials from other satisfied customers in similar situations.
4. Prove that you have a good, reliable track record for both product and company.

The Customer With a Strong Need for Popularity

These people want to be liked first and to be effective second. That means they will always be friendly and agree readily with everything you say. It will be only a superficial agreement, however. They roam from topic to topic and they avoid conflict with poor-quality compromises.

A "Popularity" executive once said that she had a problem with a particular person in her team who hadn't achieved a single financial target or stuck to the business plan. Instead of firing him, however, she promoted him to "Head of Special Projects."

How to Deal With "Popularity" Customers

1. Be positive.
2. Stress optimism.
3. Use closed questions to discourage them from talking too much.
4. Don't focus on these people unless you have to.
5. Use them as supporters for your proposals.

The Customer With a Strong Need for Self-Realization

These people take a pragmatic, flexible approach. They are solution-minded people. They tend to be self-assured but not arrogant. They are usually candid and open and will look for themes. They will not belabor points and will take risks if they feel the returns are worth it. They don't mind being proven wrong and they see differing opinions as constructive. They like constructive argument. They don't suffer fools gladly and, unfortunately, they are the customers that most salespeople like least. This is because they are very demanding and will test salespeople's beliefs. They are likely to challenge what salespeople say by asking, "Do you really believe that?" They are looking for conviction not sales talk.

"Self-Realization" customers are flexible and pragmatic, precisely the qualities that good salespeople should adopt. Salespeople should be solution-minded and results-orientated.

How to Deal With "Self-Realization" Customers

1. Stick to the point.
2. Be factual; don't use sales talk.
3. Express conviction.
4. Welcome pertinent questions.

Success in the conference room, as in any selling situation, results from preparation, planning and understanding what makes your customers tick.

How to Control the Meeting

When facing an executive board, you need to remain in control of the meeting, which means careful planning. The assistant to the top executive will always be a key player in these plans. This person sets the agenda, takes the minutes, and keeps in touch with everyone. A gold mine of information, this individual makes a useful ally. This person knows who reports to whom, who has responsibilities for different parts of the project, and who puts the final signature on the order form. The salesperson needs to know which players have a central interest in the purchase and which have only a marginal interest. This is all information that the assistant can tell you.

Make sure that you have a copy of the agenda and a list of the attendees before the meeting, and find out if the meeting has been called specifically to discuss your proposal and, if not, what its purpose is. Find out how much time you are going to have, and what questions they are likely to ask you. Ask whether they would like you to bring some technical support with you to field difficult questions. Do all the research you can on the company itself, with annual reports for the previous few years and anything else you can lay your hands on.

Build a profile of each person who will be there, including their job histories, their particular areas of expertise, and where they fit into the decision-making unit. Are they there to evaluate or to decide?

Finally, you need to know what competition you are up against and what benefits there are for the committee in saying "Yes" to your proposal or to another one.

Some decisions made in a conference room have only a marginal effect on the customer company, while others have a major effect. So you need to build a benefit bank for each player, relevant to his or her needs. You need to ascertain whether the decision is going to change the balance of power around the table.

Remember, the more research you do, the more control you will have.

Seating

You can win or lose control of the meeting by being in the right or wrong seat. Never sit in the meeting leader's seat. Look for somewhere neutral to sit, somewhere half-way down the table. Sit as far as possible from "Popularity" people, because they have the least credibility, and as near as possible to "Self-Realization" people, because they have the most credibility; you want to gain credibility by association.

Use of Names

The use of names will also help you to gain control. Introduce yourself properly and professionally. Draw up a seating plan with everyone's names to which you can refer as you make your presentation. The only reason not to use people's names is because you have forgotten them.

You can control the conversation with names, calling people in or shutting them out. "Okay, Mr. Jones," you can say, "May I direct this question at you? How many people are currently involved in this project?"

Flip Charts

A flip chart presentation is another useful way to communicate your message. If possible, make sure the flip chart is set up beforehand.

Never show what you are going to talk about until you reach the relevant point in the presentation. If you do, you will reduce dramatic impact and give the group time think about certain points out of context. Have 90 percent of the chart prepared beforehand, so that your presentation is already rehearsed. Leave 10 percent to be filled in "live" to give drama and relevance to the presentation, and to make it personal to the people in the room that day. To help you remember your points, you can prepare your charts in advance by lightly penciling in the things that you going to actually write on the flip chart in front of them later.

The Quality Close

Senior decision makers are always interested in justification, so list on your flip chart all the reasons they should buy from you, tailoring the reasons to each person around the table: the proposals to the production manager show how you will help production; the proposals to the financial officer show how you will cut costs; other managers will be interested in your added-value benefits.

You are selling the "quality" of your company, its track record, and commitment. Use references to give these senior decision makers a watertight case for using you.

Closing With Numbers

You can achieve great things with numbers, so why not use them to make your case on your flip chart.

Don't use industry norm figures, averages, or mean ratios unless you have to. Try to use the customer's own numbers, because then the committee members can't argue with them.

The best way is to develop the numbers during your presentation to the group, as you go along. For example, ask the members of the group how many people are involved, what the investment is, how many machines and so forth. Build these figures into a clear-cut case for their decision to buy from you. Work out the payback and the return on investment and cost benefits.

Often you will find that your customers are astounded because you have done something with their numbers that they had never thought of doing before.

If they can't produce the numbers you need, you should have the industry norms with you, just in case. They are much better than no numbers at all.

Concentrate on the costs, not the price, and look for angles like release of capital, reduction in waste, projected production increases, and anything that is likely to be a concern of the group.

Remember, numbers not words: you can only *read* words.

The Big-Gun Close

The big gun in this case refers to a senior member of your management team. It might be helpful to take your own manager along to the meeting with you. It could help you to control the meeting and might also encourage higher level people from the customer's company to attend. They might not have bothered had it just been a salesperson making the presentation.

Again, you will gain credibility by association. Some salespeople, due to youth or inexperience, find it difficult to sound authoritative to a group of senior people.

With your manager's support, you can call the customer contact and say, "I know you don't want me to attend this meeting, but I've mentioned it to my manager, and he would very much like to come. He says that he's got some interesting information for you that I know nothing about."

But don't ever let your ego take over. Have the confidence to ask for this big-gun help!

Using the Conference Room Mole

The mole isn't exactly a spy feeding you information, but someone around the table who is your contact. This person is more likely to be a decision influencer than a decision maker. You need to develop this person, keep in contact with him or her, and provide all the help you can. This person will help you to sell at a meeting that you cannot get invited to yourself.

The best moles are the "Security" customers, the silent ones, because when they say something on your behalf every-one will listen. "Popularity" people are the worst, because they are always talking anyway.

If you can't get into the meeting, offer your time to sit in the reception area, or on the end of the phone, in order to answer any questions that might come up. Often your contact will come out and ask you about the competition.

The conference room mole, therefore, is helping you to give feedback to a meeting even when you are not there.

The Long-Walk Close

The meeting leader may want to kick the salesperson out of the room as soon as the presentation is completed, so that the group can talk things over.

Anticipate this by going of your own accord. Once you are sure they have no more questions, volunteer to step out for a few minutes while they talk things over and tell them you will be back to answer any questions they might have. This obligates them to talk about the proposal on the spot and come up with something concrete to ask, or else they have to give you the order.

If you are able to walk out of the room without being stopped, you will more than likely close that sale, but it is a very long walk from the table to the door.

Never turn around to look at the group as you go.

13

What to Do
After You've
Closed the Sale

W hat else is there to say about closing the sale? You've won the order, the piece of paper is signed and in your briefcase. You are safe—or could you still mess it up?

Alternatively, could you actually achieve even more success from the situation? Could you turn this one successful order into three more?

There are a number of strict "don'ts" in this post-close situation:

- Don't accept a cup of tea or coffee.
- Don't keep talking about the deal—in case you talk yourself back out of it.
- Don't drop your guard.
- Don't talk about politics, gender, religion, the weather, money, sports, cars, other people, your competitors, or their competitors.

So what on earth *do* you talk about?

If customers are pushed for time, take advantage of the fact. Be considerate and leave—quickly.

If, however, customers are obviously *not* pushed for time, if they are relaxed and happy now that the big decision has been made and all their anxieties have disappeared, then you can go *fishing*.

First you must bait your hook.

"Before I go," you say casually, "I wonder if you'd do me a big favor. One of my ongoing jobs is finding people who could use this kind of equipment (or service). Do you know anyone else who might have a need?"

Or you could start fishing by asking:

"If you and I switched jobs tomorrow, who is the first person you would call on?"

Everybody likes to be helpful and to tell other people how they would do their jobs, so all you have to do is take out five blank customer records and a pen from your briefcase, and get ready to write.

As the customer provides names, write them down, checking that you get the spellings right wherever possible, or at least enough information so that you can look them up in the phone book when you get back to the office. Try to get job titles and as much information about the sort of equipment or services these people are using at the moment.

You might get only one or two names before the customer either dries up or seems to lose interest in the game. Obviously you can't push people any further than they want to go. You could try one more question, such as:

"Has anyone you know been promoted recently, gone up in the world, or taken on new responsibilities?"

Or:

"Are you a member of any trade association or professional group?"

If the answer to the last question is "Yes," then see if they can remember meeting anyone who might be interested in your products. You might ask them about their hobbies, and if, say, they play golf, whether they have met anyone down at the club recently who might be a potential customer.

If you approach this fishing technique correctly, you should be able to fill out at least three customer records, but be sure that you bring out five, because otherwise you'll never complete three. Why? Because very few customers will stop helping you until they have completed half your records. It's a kind of mental compromise. And half-way to five is three. If you used three records, most times you'd get only two of them filled in. But don't stop at three. Quite often you can get all five, sometimes even more. So have some spare copies in your briefcase.

To complete your first record you need the prospective customer's telephone number. Your existing customer may take a phone book or calendar out to give you this information. If so, watch what happens to the book *after* you've been given the number. If it stays out, chances are you might be able to get some more names.

Finally, lay the sheets out on the table and look at them. Select the one you feel is the best prospect. Pick it up.

"You said you knew George Riley well..."

"Yes."

"Could I ask you a big favor? Would you give him a call yourself for me, and ask if he has time to see me today while I'm in the area?"

If you do it right—and it does take practice—most of the customers will make the phone calls for you as well. After your customer has completed the second call you could say, "Buy you a good lunch if you call the other three."

If business results from any of these calls, go back and tell your customer, thank him or her properly, and then in three months' time you might be able to go back for more names. If you master the fishing technique, you stand a chance of getting three more successful sales from every one you make.

And you can even turn an unsuccessful close into several successful ones. If a customer gives you the "I'd like to think about it" line, then you should be able to apply what is undoubtedly one of the greatest closes ever developed.

There is a replacement-window and patio doors company that is well known for its quality and service. Here this great close is known as:

The "You're Pulling My Leg" Close

The company's salespeople go through their usual presentation, complete with samples, third-party references, photographs, measurements, and price calculations. If a customer still can't make up his or her mind, the salesperson gives a sigh of resignation and says:

"Okay, but it would be a great deal for you and your family. The value of the house would increase a lot more than the windows are going to cost. Anyway, I've done my best. Is there any chance you could help me before I go?"

The prospective customer relaxes. He or she feels let off the hook now that the salesperson is planning to go. The customer feels sufficiently guilty about taking up the salesperson's time to want to make some sort of amends.

"Sure," the customer says, "What can I do for you?"

"Do you know anyone else around here who needs replacement windows, double glazing, or patio doors?"

"Well, you could try Mr. and Mrs. Smith at Number 35. They've been talking about getting a new front door for months..."

Before you know it the customer will be telling you about all sorts of people who are improving their houses. The salesperson should get three or four really good referrals. The salesperson makes notes, checks on names, addresses, and needs, and asks if he or she can use the prospective customer's name as an introduction. Finally, the salesperson stops talking, looks down at his or her notes for a few seconds, laughs and looks back at the prospective customer.

"You're pulling my leg," the salesperson tells the customer.

"What do you mean?" the customer replies, puzzled.

"You've got to be pulling my leg. You've given me four good referrals—people you know—and you aren't going to be buying anything yourselves. You've got to be pulling my leg.

Come on, what's the real problem. Do you want to go over the numbers again?"

Eight out of ten will withdraw their stall and will buy!

This technique could work in any selling situation. It is so powerful it is a target achiever on its own.

Golden Rules

Without closing techniques your chances of making a successful sale are less than 20 percent.

- Remember, if you don't close, you're working for the competition.
- Get into the habit of closing, and *practice, practice, practice.*
- The best way to practice is to ask for an order on every call.
- It doesn't necessarily have to be *the* order, as long as it is *an* order.
- Promise yourself that you will never let a single piece of business be lost because you didn't ask for it.

So here's my closing question for you: "Will you do it?"

Index